Generation X Mindset: What Influences Their Financial and Political Decisions.

H. H. Bzozzs

Table of Content

Chapter One : Understanding The Concept Generation X
Chapter Two: Events That Shaped Generation X
Chapter Three: Generation X Characteristics
Chapter Four: Gen X and politics

Chapter One : Understanding The Concept; Generation X

Given that its members are less well recognized than those of the generations before and after, it may be appropriate that the generation positioned between baby boomers and millennials is known as "Generation X."
Since the arrival of the Beatles in the United States in 1964, their parents, the boomers, have essentially controlled popular culture.
The millennial generation, which includes their younger siblings, is praised for its use of technology, social conscience, and entrepreneurial zeal.

There are several ways to look at Generation X features.
Some, like Vanity Fair, have referred to the generation that helped create contemporary Americana culture in terms of music and art

as the one "best fitted to maintain American tradition in these gloomy new days."
The Walkmen offered America portable music, "Parental Advisory" stickers on music for the first time, modern design, and a lot more things that helped shape what America is today.

Who are the members of Generation X?
Those who were born between 1965 and 1980 are referred to as Generation Xers.
Tightly packed between loudmouth
Baby Boomers, Millennials, and Gen Xers are frequently referred to as the "middle child" of America.
Gen Xers were found to fall in the middle of just about everything, like the number of Facebook friends and patriotism, despite calling themselves the least distinct generation of the three, according to a 2014 Pew Research report that highlighted some trends between Baby Boomers, Generation X, and Millennials.

A separate study found that Gen Xers were healthier than Millennials at the same age. The fact that Generation X is financially ruinous is the spookiest trait.

While Generation X is the generation that is struggling financially the most, Millennials are because they are unable to travel or get married because of their student loan debt.

According to a recent LendingTree survey, Gen Xers have the highest average debt loads of any generation. Between 2016 and 2019, their average debt loads increased by almost 10% ($11,898).

Another interesting finding from the survey is that Gen Xers spend the most money on non-essentials like eating out and lottery tickets, but they also have the highest credit card debt of any generation.

Chapter Two: Events That Shaped Generation X

What experiences influenced the personality of Generation X?

First, it's crucial to comprehend one significant occurrence that affected many Gen Xers: the fact that many of them were latchkey kids. It's also true that the generation they belong to has the greatest divorce rates in their families. This has taught them the value of having a good dose of skepticism along with self-reliance.

The following are some significant occasions that impacted Gen Xers as they were growing up:

Berlin Wall's fall; the Challenger disaster

energy shortage

mass suicide at Jonestown

the emergence of personal computers

Watergate controversy

The bombing of the Lockerbie flight

meltdown at Three Mile Island

Employer layoffs

Rodney King assault

hostage crisis in Iran

declining the stock market

Oil tanker Exxon Valdez spill

The Desert Storm Operation

Atrocities at the Olympics in Munich

It is simpler to appreciate the flexible and occasionally skeptical mentality of Gen Xers given the unpredictability of their times. They are often referred to as the true Survivor winners.

Managers will achieve greater results from Gen X employees if they modify their strategy to take into consideration their specific generational needs.

This generation is like the middle kid in a family, unappreciated for how its members behave: hardworking, tech-savvy, educated, and independent, according to a 2014 Pew Research Center report titled "Generation X: America's Neglected "Middle Child"."

Gen Xers are less concerned with fitting in than millennials are, according to Marston, a specialist in generational change. "Millennials are herd animals and more social. They frequently take the lead from the pack in decisions.

Gen Xers, in comparison, are more prone to learn independently. They are at ease conducting research online and will review websites and social media to establish initial opinions. They are asking, "Do I like you? Marston, the creator of Generational Insights, explains, "I want to know who you truly are. They are information and people stalkers.

Kitces, the co-founder of XY Planning Network, a group of fee-only advisors who specialize in Gen X and millennial clients, notes that unlike boomers, who had the good fortune to live through years of strong market performance, Xers experienced a tech boom followed by a tech bust, followed by a real estate boom and then a global financial crash. As a result, compared to either baby boomers or millennials, this middle generation has far less faith in the markets and financial institutions.

According to Kitces, Gen Xers adhere to the maxim "Don't trust, validate" as opposed to the maxim "Trust, but verify," which was famously stated by the president of their youth, Ronald Reagan. Before they ever meet you, they will have done three or four online background checks on you to ensure that you are who you say you are and that you charge what you say you charge. They will never again have faith in you if you say something on your website that is false or deceptive.

Many advisors find it uncomfortable to undergo such extensive screening. Being pushed can be annoying, according to Kitces. But Gen Xers want to know how trustworthy you are and what you can do for them after being burned by 15 years of market stagnation and volatility.

Uncertain Investors The Census Bureau estimates that between 2007 and 2010, Gen

X investors lost over 40% of their net worth. Kol Birke, a senior vice president and financial behavior specialist at Commonwealth Financial Network, claims that individuals who neglected their investments or had the guts to "let it ride" discovered that wonderful things might come to those who wait. However, for many others, the extensive destruction-fueled the notion that sometimes nothing is safe.

Gen X is frequently hesitant to make long-term investments as a result of this terrible experience. Marston cites a 2016 Transamerica study in his book, "The Gen-Savvy Advisor: Advising the Generations in the New Age of Uncertainty," which found that four out of ten Gen Xers still felt uneasy around stocks and that nearly seven out of ten said they didn't know as much about investing as they should.

Kitces concurs. He claims that while Gen Xers have a similar underlying risk tolerance to boomers, they are less trusting of the markets. They might be willing to take risks in other ways, like investing in their own company or real estate.

Far Too Busy To Admit They Need Help

Angie Herbers, the founder of Angie Herbers LLC and columnist for Investment Advisor, argues that the actual "risk" question should be about financial security. According to that standard, she asserts that "Generation X is a high risk, unlike the preceding generations. All industries have experienced a rise in company growth, innovation, and new technologies over the previous two decades. Gen X earns more than their parents, but as a result, they risk more and have less wealth than their parents had at the same age.

Even after accounting for inflation and household size, the average Gen X household makes approximately $12,000 more than the household of their parents at the same age, according to the same Pew Research survey. In other words, Xers put in more effort than their parents did.

Less than half of Generation Xers, however, are as wealthy as their parents were when they were their age. You can blame a later start in life because of longer schooling, a lower savings rate, and less market cooperation. For many members of this generation, "smaller savings" should be substituted by "greater student debt."

Regarding market volatility, according to Noah Smith on Bloomberg View, Gen Xers witnessed gains of only 1.9% from 2000 to 2014, which is far lower than boomers, whose portfolios were boosted by the S&P 500's 15.4% real annualized return between 1985 and 2000.

The Unknown World of Finance

Herbers asserts that there is a more serious problem. She claims that as a Gen Xer, "Our generation is apathetic to talking about money," in contrast to "millennials who talk about money all the time" and "boomers who avoid talking about money."

This does not imply that Gen Xers are unconcerned with money. Herbers affirms, "We do care." Simply put, "We need help since we frequently don't know what to do with money or where to turn.

She thinks that Gen Xers frequently lack preparation in many financial aspects of their lives because of this lack of awareness. She notes that research indicates they have inadequate insurance, inadequate retirement savings, and no financial literacy instruction for their children. They lack confidence in general when it comes to money since they see it to be insignificant due to their lack of knowledge of it.

What Are They Looking For?

According to Herbers, there is a distinct difference between the messages that each generation likes to hear. "Baby boomers prefer blunt communication. Millennials prefer messages that have a dynamic feel to them. Gen X prefers messages that have a purpose.

The greatest way to get over apathy, she says, is to find significance. "You have to question them, 'What does money mean to you?' to break them out of their indifference and make them care more about money. Gen X requires assistance in understanding the purpose of their money, in contrast to millennials who find meaning in social issues and baby boomers who made money their meaning.

What advice would therefore be most effective with this generation? Anything that serves a function, Herbers responds.

Trust is crucial because it fosters a high level of loyalty in millennials. Although Gen Xers frequently choose independent decisions, Marston notes that they do have pals with whom they may give wise counsel and suggestions for reliable individuals. However, if they believe they have been duped, their devotion can go in an instant.

The behavior of Generation Xers varies as they gain financial literacy. According to a 2016 Transamerica Institute report, 52% of Xers who used advisors had at least $100,000 saved for retirement. Of those without a financial counselor, only 27% had saved that much.

Children of this generation can also benefit from improved financial literacy. This generation has begun to recognize the peril of keeping mute about money, according to Birke, much as they were conscious of the need to fasten their children's seatbelts and wear bicycle helmets. "Much more parents seem to be emphasizing money conversations with their kids than their boomer parents did, even though it's still awkward for those who don't feel they have a handle on the subject themselves," according to the study.

He continues, "Money is still a personal, taboo, and for the majority, frightening subject. The more open and honest they can be with their friends and loved ones about their finances, the better off this generation will be. This, in my opinion, is the greatest gift they can give their children.

The problem for advisers, according to Gen Xer Herbers, is to achieve that cross-generational benefit. Despite having a smaller population than either of their parent generations—roughly 65 million Xers compared to 77 million boomers and 83 million millennials—she asserts that this generation will define financial advice. And the Gen X generation currently needs financial assistance more than any other.

Chapter Three: Generation X Characteristics

Independent: This generation is also known as the latchkey generation or the latchkey kids. These terms were employed since several of them, as a result of their parents' dual employment or other circumstances, arrived home by themselves after school. This upbringing may have encouraged the independence that we see in Generation X today.

Flexible: Generation Xers have experienced some of history's greatest significant societal transformations and advancements. They developed flexibility, readiness for change when it occurs, and the ability to deal with it out of necessity. As Gen Xers questioned cultural traditions like why a suit was required for some positions or why some communication was so formal, this flexibility (coupled with critical thinking) also led to changes in communication, workplace environments, and culture.

Critical Thinkers: Although some have characterized Generation X as cynical, it may be more accurate to describe them as critical thinkers. Like other generations, Gen X was educated to a higher level than its predecessor and grew up in a period of intense social division. Generation X has good reason to consider the world critically because of the divisive Vietnam War and the Watergate scandal.

Self-Reliant: Gen Xers learned to rely on themselves and make the most of their circumstances, which is similar to how independent they were. They didn't always have the best outlook on the future because they had grown up with the prospect of nuclear war hanging over their heads, but they were determined to change the world and carve out a place for themselves.

Chapter Four: Gen X and politics

The generation known as Gen X, which was generally defined as individuals born between 1965 and 1980, reached adulthood during the administration of President Ronald Reagan and the conclusion of the Cold War. The common perception of Generation X has never exactly fit into any straightforward political framework. It is the generation that gave rise to gangsta rap and grunge music, as well as the 1980s "greed is good" era immortalized in Oliver Stone's Wall Street. In actuality, the most common perception of this generation's politics was that they were nonpartisan. Except for generic skepticism and MTV's "Choose or Lose" campaign, which aimed to persuade young voters that politics even matter, the slackers portrayed in Richard Linklater movies or the grunge rockers in flannel were essentially devoid of any political tendency.

Although exit poll data doesn't always show a distinct generational division, they fluctuated in presidential elections after their initial victory in 1984 but were never particularly progressive and tended to lean to the right of the country as a whole.

Even if they were sometimes hidden by the less politically charged environment at the time, there were always clues of a more right-wing cultural bent. The comedy Family Ties had Reagan-supporting youngster Alex P. Keaton at odds with his liberal baby boomer parents in the first significant political representation of this generation. "The MTV generation has always been a little bit more conservative," Republican pollster Patrick Ruffini told Politico.

But as of right now, there is no doubt that Generation X is a reliable Republican.

The mid-to-late 1960s generation is the most Republican-leaning group overall, more so than the older Boomers and Silent generation, according to a 2014 model that only included white voters through the 2012 election. Generation X had the highest degree of disdain for Biden and was the generation most likely to indicate they would vote for a Republican candidate in the midterm elections if they were held that day, according to a poll issued in late April by Marist/NPR.

Although older voters have typically tended to be more conservative, this trend has accelerated with the emergence of Generation X. In fact, Generation X has surpassed the Baby Boomers in terms of conservatism, according to Tom Bonier, CEO of Democratic data company TargetSmart.

A portion of this is related to more general historical forces that were beyond anyone's control. Voters' lives are affected by the political climate in which they first cast ballots and first became politically aware. If you first become interested in politics during the Reagan/[George H.W.] Bush/Clinton era, you're more likely to lean a little further to the right, according to Republican pollster Kristen Soltis Anderson. Even Bill Clinton was saying at the time that "the age of big government is ended."

Westrich, who was born in 1966, belongs to the oldest and, in some analyses, the most traditional group within this generation. She would have reached voting age at a time when few prominent figures were defining the Democratic Party, and the first presidential election she would have been able to vote in was Reagan's resounding victory in 1984. Reagan's performance among voters under 30 improved by 15 percentage points over 1980, according to exit polls from that year, which was the highest improvement in any single group at the time.

The 1990s were also not very political years for Westrich. On the tour bus, there was no discussion of Hillarycare or Newt Gingrich. Instead, it was a nerdy nomadic journey across many cities and nations. Westrich and fellow keyboardist Maya Rudolph, who subsequently rose to fame on Saturday Night Live, would shoot comedic videos on their Super 8 camera in place of political discourse.

Even her decision to join the band came about as a result of several mishaps. It was a side project of Weezer bassist Matt Sharp. Sharp saw some lull in the year before the Blue Album, the breakout debut from Weezer was released. He put some friends together and recorded a demo on it. Once it was in the hands of a small punk rock label, they showed interest. Westrich was one of the two buddies whom Sharp recruited to pose as the band responsible for the demo.

It worked, and the two began producing an album before ever performing live together, along with Weezer drummer Patrick Wilson and the guitarist from Westrich's band at the time, Rod Cervera.

As a result, Ronnie James Dio, the former lead singer of Black Sabbath, who was also recording at the same location, observed numerous rehearsals at a studio that were occasionally interrupted by games of hacky sack.

Westrich was then more notable for her interest in restoring classic cars than for any political leanings. Sharp remembered that "in the alternative environment of 1995, there weren't too many Moog-playing, mechanically inclined synthesizer musicians."

Sharp had very little memory of participating in politics at the time. "I don't think any of us were too engaged in such stuff because we were quite young and had other things on our thoughts," one of us said.

Westrich also couldn't recollect any political discussion. She remarked that she "felt like politics was for rich people" at the time. She remarked, "I just thought that was never going to be for me because I grew up... without a lot of money because everyone in politics had money. Before Trump, she couldn't even think of a single candidate who had truly motivated her, and she characterized her prior voting as being "choosing between the lesser of two evils" and frequently consisting of voting against incumbents from both parties.
Westrich didn't become involved in politics until 2016.

She recently relocated to Ottumwa, Iowa, to be with her long-term partner, and a friend she worked out with persuaded her to volunteer for Trump's general election campaign. "She was talking about making phone calls and knocking on doors for Trump and urging me to attend, and I kept saying 'no thanks,'" Westrich recalled.
But eventually, she gave in and went to the Trump campaign office.

She discovered that she enjoyed conversing with voters. She remarked, "It was fun talking to individuals, and I appreciated being able to provide them with useful information. Regarding the voters she spoke with, she claimed that "they weren't doing their homework." They felt informed since they watched the evening news, but they couldn't go any further.

The political environment largely disregards Generation X because it is one of the smaller generations.

The two main groups vying for political influence are the Millennials and the Baby Boomers (Currier,2018). Baby Boomers and the Silent Generation both produced several American Presidents,

Generation X hasn't done it yet. However, this is probably because only a very small part of that group would have even been allowed to run for president due to age, and many Millennials in politics are still just beginning their careers. Millennials have not yet had a president who belongs to their generation. Generation X's absence is not particularly noticeable in the political sphere, giving the impression that they are relatively detached from it. They appear to somewhat bridge the gap between the conservative fervor of many Baby Boomers and the leftward trend of

Millennials. They are more accepting of the growing diversity in the US and hold more liberal social viewpoints than Baby Boomers, although they do not exhibit as many liberal tendencies as Millennials (Pew Research Center, 2011). Additionally, it appears that the political environment in which Generation X was raised has influenced their opinions. The older generation of Generation X, which first engaged in politics under the Reagan and Bush administrations, has tended to favor Republicans more than the general populace. However, younger members of Generation X who were able to vote during the Clinton administration have generally voted more Democratic than the general electorate (Pew Research Center, 2011). Therefore,

Due to their party split and tendency to melt into the political background, Generation X is a little more of a mixed bag than other generations.

www.ingramcontent.com/pod-product-compliance
Lightning Source LLC
LaVergne TN
LVHW052113160826
845678LV00015B/3526

* 9 7 9 8 3 5 9 3 3 1 3 2 6 *